It Rained All Day that Night

Autographs, Rhymes & Inscriptions

compiled by **Lillian Morrison**

illustrated by **Christy Hale**

August House Publishers, Inc.

LITTLE ROCK

In memory of Margaret—LM

For my childhood best friend Leslie Meredith Bates—CH

Text © 2003 by Lillian Morrison
Illustrations © 2003 by Christy Hale

Published 2003 by August House Publishers, Inc.,
P.O. Box 3223, Little Rock, Arkansas 72203,
501-372-5450
www.augusthouse.com

Book design by Christy Hale
Manufactured in Korea
10 9 8 7 6 5 4 3 2 1 HB
10 9 8 7 6 5 4 3 2 1 PB

Library of Congress Cataloging-in-Publication Data
It rained all day that night : autograph album verses and inscriptions / compiled
by Lillian Morrison ; illustrated by Christy Hale.
Summary: An illustrated compilation of short poems and other inscriptions from
autograph albums, arranged by such themes as friendship, school, and nonsense.
ISBN 0-87483-735-9 (alk. paper) —ISBN 0-87483-726-X (pbk : alk. paper)
1. Autograph albums—Juvenile literature. 2. Autograph verse. 3. Children's poetry,
American. [1. Autograph albums. 2. Poetry—Collections.] I. Morrison, Lillian.
II. Hale, Christy, ill.
Z41.I8 2003
081—dc21   2003051987

contents

Love your friends, love them well,
But to your friends no secrets tell;
For if your friend becomes your foe
Your secrets everyone will know.

Ashes to ashes,
Dust to dust.
You're one friend
That I can trust.

ITALY
(I Trust and Love You)

When you're sitting all alone
Thinking of the past,
Remember there is one true friend
Whose love will always last.

HOLLAND

Hope Our Love Lasts And Never Dies

I'm proud of the country I live in,
I'm proud of the red, white, and blue.
I'm proud to have a good friend
As sweet and nice as you.

Columbus discovered America
In 1492,
And I discovered a great friend
When I discovered you.

There are golden ships,
There are silver ships,
But the best ship
Is Friendship.

2 good
2 B
2 soon
<u>4</u> got
10

Here's champagne to
our real friends
And real pain
to our sham friends.

There is White Rose te
There is Ceylon tea,
But there's no tea
Like loyalty.

Those friends are dearest
Who stand by us nearest,
Who lend us their aid
When our hopes slowly fade.

A F A
(A Friend Always)

Though days be dark
And friends be few,
Remember me
And I will you.

I've seen you in the morning,
I've seen you in the night,
I've seen you quite a lot of times
And we've never had a fight.

Yours in friendship,
Yours in fun,
Yours in everything
Under the sun.

B F F
(Best Friend Forever)

f you get to Heaven
Before I do,
Tell St. Peter
I'm coming too.

If you get to Heaven before I do,
Bore a little hole
and
pull
me
through.

When a feather weighs a pound,
When a fox shall chase a hound,
When the world comes to an end,
Then I shall cease to be your friend.

In the golden chain of friendship, consider me a link.

As long as grapes grow on a vine

You'll always be a friend of mine.

In your ocean of friends, please count me as a permanent wave.

Sometimes a tie is round your neck
And sometimes in a railroad track.
But best the tie that makes us friends
When school-day memories come back.

Friendship is like china—
Costly and rare.
Though it can be mended
The scratches are still there.

True friends are like diamonds,
Precious but rare;
False friends are like autumn leaves,
Scattered everywhere.

There are three things you must learn to do:
Lie in the bed of success.
Steal away from bad company.
Drink from the fountain of youth.

Judge—Amanda
Court—Forest Park School
Prisoner—Stuart
Cell—Mrs. Simpson's home room
Crime—Graduation
Sentence—A life of success and happiness

May your life be like an old-fashioned gown:
Long and beautiful.

May you always meet Dame Fortune
But never her daughter, Miss Fortune.

Always be like a piano: grand and upright.

Best of luck in junior high.

High.

Climb

Low

Start

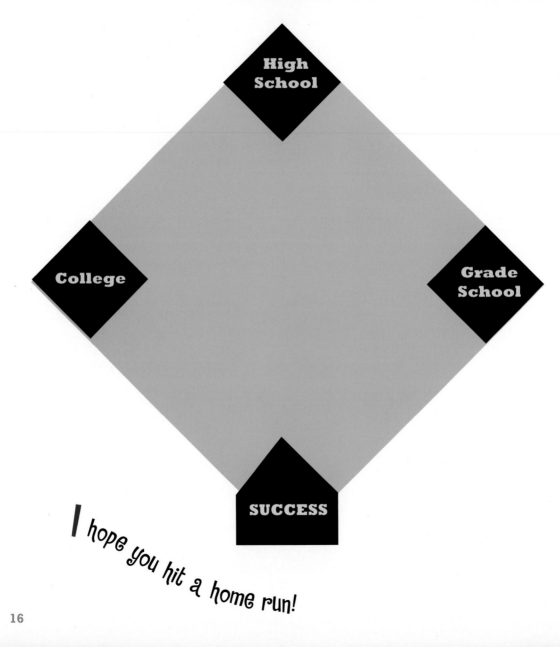

He that takes but never gives
May last for years but never lives.

Dream as if you will live forever.
Live as if you will die tomorrow.

Though the tasks are many
And your rewards are few,
Remember that the mighty oak
Was once a nut like you.

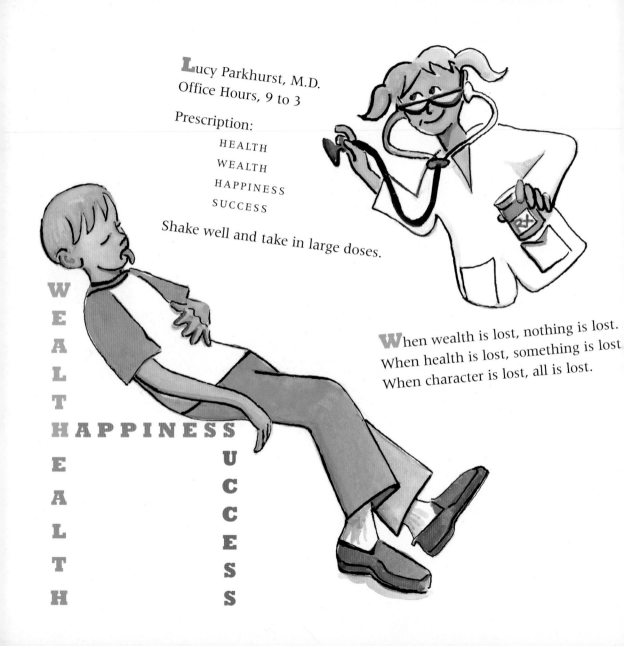

Lucy Parkhurst, M.D.
Office Hours, 9 to 3

Prescription:

HEALTH
WEALTH
HAPPINESS
SUCCESS

Shake well and take in large doses.

When wealth is lost, nothing is lost.
When health is lost, something is lost.
When character is lost, all is lost.

Never B♯
Never B♭
Always B♮

top.
the
at
room
always
is
There

Never trouble trouble
Till trouble troubles you.

There is free cheese
in every trap.

Don't be ～ (crooked)
Don't be + (cross)
Just be ____ (straight)
And you'll be boss.

When you are in love it is ♥
When you are engaged it is ♦
When you are married it is ♣
When you are dead it is ♠

The past is a dream,
The present a strife,
The future a mystery,
And such is life.

It's nice to be natural
If you're naturally nice.

May you live
as long as you want
And never want
as long as you live.

If your shoe is in a knot
Patience will untie it.
Patience will do many things.
Did you ever try it?

May your life be like spaghetti:
long and full of dough.

Never frown, even when you are sad.
You never know when someone is
falling in love with your smile.

May your heart be as light as a snowflake.
May your troubles dissolve like them too.
And a snowstorm of good wishes
I'm hoping will fall on you.

Yesterday's history,
Tomorrow's a mystery,
Today's a gift—
That's why they call it the present.

May your luck be like the capital of Ireland:
Always Dublin.

May your past be *A Midsummer Night's Dream*
And your future *As You Like It.*

Through fear of taking risks in life
I've missed a lot of fun.
The only things that I regret
Are the things I haven't done.

May your future be as bright
As Broadway at night
And your heart be as true
As the red, white, and blue.

Don't wait for
your ship to come in.
Row out and meet it.

Remember the Homework that Never Got Done

School

May your life be like math:

Joys + (added)
Sorrows − (subtracted)
Happiness × (multiplied)
Love Un ÷ (divided)

I am Perfec!

Remember **A**
Remember **B**
Remember the day
We both got **D**.

I wasn't late.
The bell was early.

Remember the fights,
Remember the fun,
Remember the homework
That never got done.

You can drive a
horse to water
But a pencil must
be lead.

Remember **A**
Remember **B**,
But **C** that **U**
Remember me.

A B C
Ability, Brains, and Charm

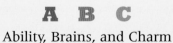

The Test
I know the answers
from A to Z.
It's just the middle
that's worrying me.

Now I lay me down to rest,
I pray I pass tomorrow's test.
If I die before I wake,
That's one less test I'll have to take.

Work never killed anyone—
But I'm not taking a chance.

Latin is a dead language,
It's plain enough to see.
It killed off all the Romans,
And now it's killing me.

Friends, Romans, classmates—
Lend me your homework.

RECOMMENDED READING
I Fell Over the Cliff by Eileen Dover
Jump Over the Cliff by Hugo Furst

Row, row, row your boat
Gently down the stream.
Throw Mrs. Vogel overboard
And listen to her scream.

Come Out of Your Coma

Insults

Roses are red,
Violets are blue.
The sidewalk is cracked,
And so are you.

Roses are red,
Violets are blue.
St. Joseph's is glad
To get rid of you.

Roses are red,
Pickles are green.
My face is a holler,
But yours is a scream.

Roses are red,
Violets are blue.
Let's hope the teachers
Keep passing you.

Roses are red,
Violets are blue.
God made me pretty—
What happened to you?

Over the hill there is a school
And in that school there is a room
And in that room there is a stool
And on that stool there is a fool
And the fool is named Drew Bailey.

Don't feel that you're useless.
We can always use you as a bad example

While Greenville Middle is getting a rest
Greenville High is getting a pest.

Found a raindrop
Found a raindrop
Found a raindrop in the sky.
But I'd rather
Be a raindrop
Than a drip from Tully High.

Poor little Travis
Sitting on a fence,
Trying to get to middle school
Without any sense.

```
O   U   R
2   rot   10
2   B
———————————
4   got   10
```

You could go far.
Why don't you?

2   4   6   8
Who do we appreciate?
The teachers of P.S. 2
Who finally pulled
Jonathan through.

ome out of your coma
nd get your diploma.

East is East,
West is West,
St. Joseph's is getting
Rid of a pest.

I'm Cliff.
Drop over sometime.

enerally speaking,
cy's generally speaking.

2   4   6   8
How the heck did you graduate?

I'm the king of the castle
And you're a dirty rascal.

Just because your head is shaped
like an air conditioner
Doesn't mean you're so cool.

Don't worry if you're a little cracked.
The Liberty Bell is, too.

You remind me of a puzzle—
all mixed up.

You remind me of London—
always in a fog.

You love yourself, you think you're grand.
You go the movies and hold your hand.
You put your arm around your waist,
And when you get fresh you slap your face.

With This Pen I Write My Name

Inscriptions

When you are dying
And making your will
Remember the one
Who wrote uphill.

Can't think,
Brain dumb.
Inspiration
Just won't come.
Poor ink,
Bum pen,
Best wishes,
Amen.

As years roll by,
As years surely will,
Remember your friend
Who wrote downhill.

Roses are red, green grow the hedges, I hope you don't mind me writing on the edges.

The owner of this book has asked
1   2   3   4   5   6   7
A word or two of me,
8   9   10   11   12   13
But being in a generous mood
14   15   16 17   18   19
I've written twenty-three.
20   21   22   23

My ink is pale,
My pen is frail,
My hand shakes like
A puppy's tail.

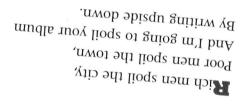

Rich men spoil the city,
Poor men spoil the town,
And I'm going to spoil your album
By writing upside down.

Best wishes too you
From the kid who couldn't spell.

I was here and am now gone.
I'll leave my name to carry on.

Autograph signing is rather tough;
Here's my name, and that's enough.

Just to make you angry,
Just to make you frown,
I'm writing in your album
Upside down.

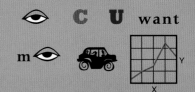

Until I learn to write,
this is all I have to say.

2 Ys **U R**
2 Ys **U B**
I C U R
2 Ys **4** me

This is a period.
This is a dot ●
This is a star ★
This is a blot
Forget me not.

Remember **A**
Remember **B**,
But **C** that **U**
Remember me.

This is Page One
And just for fun
I'll begin the text
By writing my "**X**."

C U want

O U Q T
I N V U

You think you're smart,
You think you're fine.
But I'll bet you can't sign
Your name under mine.

Aimee Stockton

When months and years have glided by
And on this page you cast your eye
Remember it was a friend sincere
Who signed her name on this page here.

When on this page
You chance to look
Just think of me
And close the book.

44

When on this page your eyes do end
Think of me always as your friend.

When I am gone out of your mind
Within this book my name you'll find,
And when my name you plainly see
You will then remember me.

45

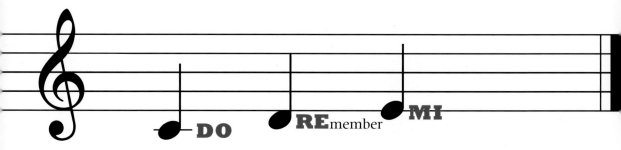

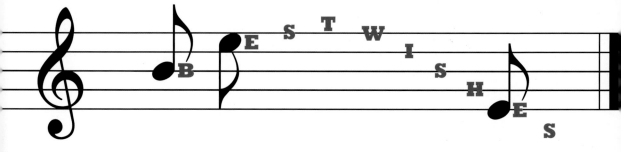

When I am dead and in my grave
And all my bones are rotten,
This little book will bear my name,
Which long has been forgotten.

Gracie Burruss is my name
And with this pen I write the same.
The grass is green, the rose is red;
Remember me when I am dead.

I'm the clown
Who came to town
And signed your album
Upside down.

The Four Corners of the Round Table

Nonsense

I climbed up the door
And shut the stairs.
I said my shoes
And took off my prayers.
I shut off the bed
And climbed into the light,
And all because he kissed me goodnight.

Said the toe to the sock,
"Let me through, let me through."
Said the sock to the toe,
"I'll be darned if I do."

Coca-Cola came to town.
Pepsi-Cola shot him down.
Dr. Pepper fixed them up.
Now they all drink 7-Up.

One fine day in the middle of the night
Two dead men got up to fight.
One was a clown, and the other was a goon.
They fought all day that night till noon.

Ladies and gentlemen,
Hobos and tramps,
Cross-eyed mosquitoes
And bow-legged ants
I come before you to stand behind you
To tell you a story I know nothing about.
Late Thursday night, early Friday morning
An empty truck full of bricks
Pulled into my front yard,
Killing my cat in the back yard.
That same night two boys got up to fight.
Back to back they faced one another.
A deaf policeman heard the noise,
Came and shot the two dead boys.
If you don't believe this lie is true,
Ask the blind man—
He saw it too.

Ladies and gentlemen,
I come before you to stand behind you,
to tell you something I know nothing about.
Next Thursday, which is Good Friday,
there will be a meeting of the Ladies Club for men only.
Admission is free, pay at the door,
pull up a chair and sit on the floor.
The next meeting will be held
at the four corners of the round table.

Ladies and jellybeans,
Reptiles and crocodiles,
I stand before you to sit behind you
To tell you something I know nothing about.
There will be a meeting tomorrow evening
Right after breakfast
To decide which color to whitewash the church.
There is no admission
So pay at the door.
There are plenty of seats
So sit on the floor.

I saw you in the ocean,
I saw you in the sea.
I saw you in the bathtub—
Oops, pardon me!

It's hard to lose a friend
When your heart is full of hope,
But it's worse to lose a towel
When your eyes are full of soap.

Humpty Dumpty sat on a wall,
Humpty Dumpty had a great fall.
All the king's horses and all the king's men
Had scrambled eggs for breakfast again.

Hickory, dickory, dock,
The mice ran up the clock.
The clock struck one;
The others escaped with minor injuries.

Mary had a little lamb.
Its fleece was white as snow.
Mary passed a butcher shop
But the lamb went by too slow.

A tree toad loved a she toad
That lived up in a tree.
She was a three-toed tree toad
But a two-toed toad was he.
The two-toed tree toad tried to win
The she toad's friendly nod,
For the two-toed tree toad loved the ground
That the three-toad tree toad trod.
But vainly the two-toed tree toad tried.
He could not please her whim.
In her tree toad bower
With her V-toed power
The she toad vetoed him.

I was sitting on a tombstone,
And a ghost came and said,
"Sorry to disturb you,
But you're sitting on my head."

It was midnight on the ocean.
Not a streetcar was in sight.
The sun was shining brightly,
For it rained all day that night.
It was a summer day in winter,
And snow was raining fast
As a barefoot boy with shoes on
Stood sitting on the grass.

The rain came down with an awful thud
And said to the dust, "Your name is mud."

57

Roses are red,
Violets are blue.
Unless you have a garden
That won't affect you.

Roses are red,
Violets are blue.
Orchids are fifty bucks.
Will dandelions do?

City of Love, State of Wishes

Love, Boys & Marriage

You can fall from the mountains,
You can fall from above.
But the best way to fall
Is to fall in love.

When you fall in the river, there is a boat;
When you fall in a well, there is a rope;
When you fall in love, there is no hope.

Fall from a steamer's burning deck,
Fall from a horse and break your neck,
Fall from the starry skies above,
But never, never fall in love.

Beware of boys with eyes of brown;
They kiss you once and turn you down.
Beware of boys with eyes of blue;
They kiss you once and ask for two.
Beware of boys with eyes of gray;
They kiss you once and turn away.
Beware of boys with eyes of black;
They kiss you once and never come back.
You will know all kinds of joys
If only you'll beware of boys.

You're a very religious girl—
always saying, "Ah, men."

Our eyes have met,
Our lips not yet,
But oh you kid,
I'll get you yet.

Be | good as a Christian
Wise | as a saint
And | when the boy asks you to
Kiss | him, tell
Him | you can't.

My  4 U.

(My heart pants for you.)

City of Love
State of Wishes
19 Hugs
74 Kisses

Read   see   that   r
up   will   I   lo
and   you   love   y
down   and   you   a

2
2
4   young
    go
    boys

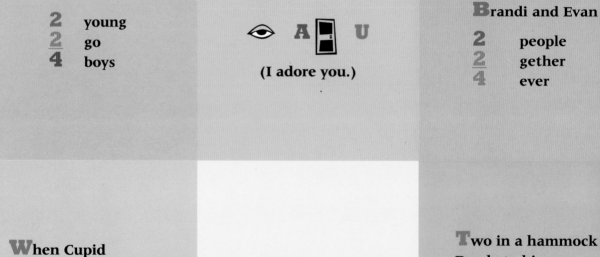

👁 **A** 🚪 **U**

(I adore you.)

Brandi and Evan

2
2
4   people
    gether
    ever

When Cupid
shoots his arrow,
I hope he **Mrs.** you.

I pine fir yew.

Two in a hammock
Ready to kiss,
When all of a sudden
It went like this!

You are a peach.

If we cantaloupe,

Lettuce marry;

Weed make a swell pear.

If a boy tries to win your ♥
Make sure he gives you ♦
If he is untrue, hit him with a ♣
And let the undertaker use the ♠

Girls' faults are many,
Boys have only two—
Everything they say
And everything they do.

When sailing never quarrel
For you'll find without a doubt
A boat is not a proper place
To have a falling-out.

Remember this, and bear in mind,
A good man is hard to find;
But when you fine one good and true
Stick to him like Elmer's Glue.

Megan is your name,
Single is your station.
Happy is the lucky man
Who makes the alteration.

When you get married,
Let your husband run things
around your house:
  the vacuum cleaner …
  the washing machine …
  the dishwasher …

When your husband is thirsty
And wants a drink,
Take him to the kitchen
And show him the sink.

When you are married
And live in New York,
Don't open the door.
It may be the stork.

When you get married
And live across the sea,
Send me a sailor
C.O.D.

When you are married
And have eight or nine,
Bundle them up
And come to see mine.

Pins and needles,
Needles and pins,
Don't get excited
When the doctor says, "Twins!"

the m
to hea
becon

Your heart is not a plaything,
Your heart is not a toy.
But if you want it broken
Just give it to a boy.

Yours Till the Kitchen Sinks

One-liners

Yours till...

...soda pops

...butter flies

...Britney spears

...Dracula stops being a pain in the neck

...cigars box

...ginger snaps

...the barn dances and the fire escapes

...the kitchen sinks

...meatballs bounce

...the U.S. drinks Canada dry

...the Cats kill Mountains

...cat fishes

...the mountain peeks and sees the salad dressing

71

Yours till...

...Niagara Falls

...the catfish has kittens

...Gaza strips

...they feed the corn on your toes to the calves on your legs

...the tree develops square roots

...the toilet bowls

...the pencil case is solved

...ice skates

...the sidewalks

...the trees pack their trunks

...the board walks

...the river Seine becomes insane

LOUISIANA

MISSISSIPPI

...lemon drops

...the mouth of the
Mississippi wears lipstick

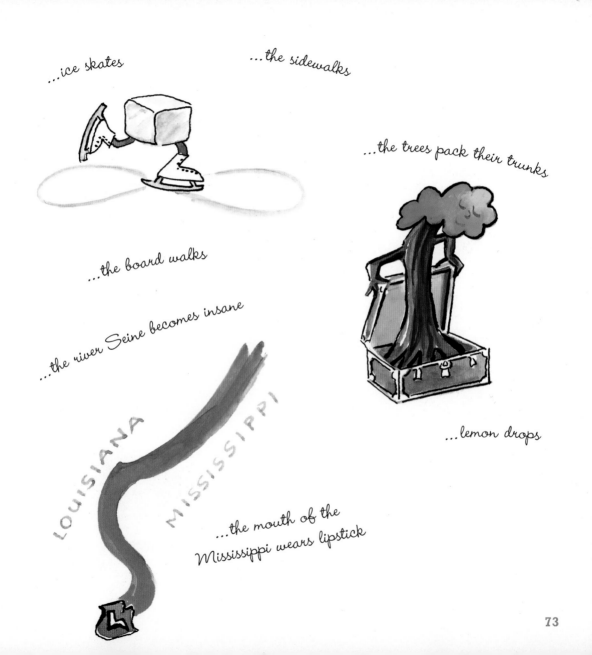

Yours till...

...dogwood barks

...the cereal bowls

...cement walks

...horse flies

...the pillowcase goes to court

...the radio waves

...the bed spreads

...Dawson creaks

...the sawhorse has colts

...Russia cooks Turkey in Greece and serves it on China to the Hungary

...ice screams

...potato chips, the ferry slips, and the comic strips

Yours till the end.

This is the end.

Afterword

Today's children have much to occupy their time in this electronic age with its rapid technological advances. They watch television, videocassettes, and DVDs; they play video games; they listen to popular music on CDs and MP3s. Some do their homework on computers and communicate by e-mail and instant message. Yet, surprisingly, the custom of writing in longhand in yearbooks and memory books still persists. Perhaps it is not surprising after all, because it is children, the preservers of folklore, who keep alive many old, formerly adult customs, in their own inventive and fun-loving ways.

Writing in autograph albums is indeed an old custom. It began in mid-sixteenth century Europe among university students who traveled from learning center to learning center carrying the leather-bound *album amicorum* (book of friends), as it was called. Friends, patrons, and professors would write in it their recommendations, good wishes, and words of wisdom, usually in the form of literary quotations and often in Latin or Greek. Many such albums can be found today in the British Museum in London.

In America, albums began to appear in great numbers in the 1820s and 1830s, probably brought over by European immigrants in those years. By the late nineteenth century, they had become increasingly popular with young women in their late teens and twenties who would pass their books around at parties to be signed by friends—male and female. The pages were often decorated with floral designs, and those signers who could showed off their elaborate penmanship. For those who were unable to write something original, printed collections, such as *The Album Writer's Friend,* filled with sentimental and moralistic verse, were available.

The postcard-shaped albums of the century just past, sold in stationery stores and popular with eighth-graders soon to enter high school, can now be found in many a bureau drawer and attic. These days it seems to be early middle-schoolers and older elementary students, using notebooks of various shapes and sizes, who keep the custom going, asking schoolmates, campmates, friends, and relations for their written messages to be remembered by.

Not only have the album owners become younger over the years, but the type of verse inscribed has undergone definite changes. You will seldom find a literary quotation or overly didactic or sentimental verse today. The style tends to be direct, down-to-earth, often mocking, humorous, impudent—sometimes sweet, sometimes nonsensical. Some of the verses are original with the writer, but many appear in albums again and again, with variations. The verse *Roses are red/Violets are blue/The pink is pretty/And so are you,* which has been traced to Elizabethan times, has spawned hundreds of variants that appear today. Other verses from previous times continue to appear because they have an appealing vitality that keeps them fresh.

Essentially, writing in autograph albums is about friendship, fun, and remembering. So it is especially satisfying, in these times of media overload and commercial messages, that this very human, face-to-face custom survives, as do these catchy rhymes and inscriptions expressing the warmth, humor, and irrepressible spirit of the young.

I have enjoyed collecting autograph album verses and sayings for decades—ever since rereading my own eighth-grade album many years ago. This book is a potpourri containing not only selections from three of my previously published collections (all long out-of-print) but many newly collected pieces as well. For some of the latter, I especially wish to thank the following students from the central Arkansas area: Megan Fausett, Mary Helen Marks, Diana Montez, Laura Panozzo, Lucy Parkhurst, and Jasmine Williams.

I am grateful as well to all the people who have kindly lent me albums or contributed verses over the years: friends, relatives, friend's friends, and my former colleagues in The New York Public Library, particularly in the Office of Young Adult Services and in the Aguilar, Nathan Straus, and Kingsbridge branches. And last, but by no means least, my special thanks to the many children and teenagers with whom I came in contact in my years as a librarian and who contributed so much.

—Lillian Morrison